Words in Echo

Words in Echo

A Chichimeca Symphony

Rudy Gallardo

Acknowledgments

Writing is an intrinsic process that requires acts of self concentrative silence. However, it is a not a solitary process, but a community of people that nourish it. Therefore, I wish to express my appreciation for that nourishment to Morris Martinez, Fernando and Olga Hernandez, Mary Ellen Barker, Larry Anderson, Arllynne Hall and family, Victoria Rocha, Al Herrera, Rebecca Mendoza, Juan and Ana Montes-Gonzales, Anita and John Rodelo, Diana Martinez and her deceased husband, Carlos, Teri and Curt Stock, Raul Pickett, John and America Martinez, Alyce Lawr, John and Kathy Garcia, Nash Lopez, Victoria Filgas, Hector and Gloria Cortes. And to my immediate family: Sheila, Feliciano, Gauge, Xavier, Rosa and Alfredo Gallardo, and to all the Gallardos in Denair, as well as to the Gallardos from Tennessee, Hawaii, Alaska and Nevada, Cristal Yepez, and Raina, Caesar, Stacy, and Marisela de la Cruz. Though, lastly and with high regard and appreciation to my editors, who for sure this work would not have been possible, Jorge George Verdugo, and Dr. Jorge Garcia.

Historical Blurb

It has been said that Rudy Gallardo's mother, a beautiful Chichimecha maiden, was kidnapped at knife point while she was at the river retrieving water for her family. This did not happen in pre-columbian times or even centuries ago; this happened in these modern times. This is the world, of humble beginnings, that Rudy was born into. There were no silver spoons; likely no spoons at all.

Because of his mother's hard work, courage, discipline, and love for her children, she moved the family northward to the United States of America, settling in Merced. A town in California's Central San Joaquin Valley, and using it as a base to traverse it, looking for farm work in its agricultural fields.

Despite his humble beginnings, and in the face of bias and discrimination, Rudy never gave up on his desire to improve his life. His accomplishments are extraordinary given the obstacles he had to overcome.

Like his mother, his role model, he worked hard in pursuit of his education. Eventually he earned his bachelor's degree and went on to teach literature and writing at CSU Fresno where he earned his degree and at San Francisco State university. He also taught and lectured for the San Francisco community college district.

Rudy's work has been published by Scott Foresman & Son, Houghton & Mifflin, Canfield Press and in other publications: Tin Tan, El Tecolote, Poets, Cock Roaches, and Flies, and in The Commons, a CSU Fresno student publication.

Next to writing, his involvement in community development has been the love and focus of his life.

Rudy Gallardo's visionary poetry is written from his life experiences and observations.

Dedication

This book is dedicated to my wife, Sheila Cortez Gallardo and to my mother, Guadalupe Regalado Gallardo de Escalera.

BOLEROS

Pastels & Life

Waiting for an image
to appear and disappear:
to dissipate into a pebble
of snow, into a vacuum of
space (like a wind
            swollen with glare).

Waiting for the horizon,
and, for eternity's light to
dissolve the cries of violence
and forlorn anticipations...

Waiting for words
like in a peony flower, to
decorate the history of time,
   so that the palm
can stretch beyond its
         fingertips,
and design a meticulous
yawn, coloring the sheen
         of your hair.

Lupe Gallardo
Mother

Wet with sorrow
The rain splashes on
The leaves of a

       Fern.

The wind,
A gale from
The sea...

Sobs like an
Abandoned violin,
And my voice,
A mist in

Faraway places
Seeks your face

In ruffled forests,
In twigs and tulips,

And in the roses
That grow

       in the rain

Coffee Words

Words floating in space intrigue me.
They come wet with saliva and hunger,
Or hang suspended in my hands.
They walk me to the coffee pot in the
Kitchen and to the strange mysteries
Of the beyond, under and above the
Timelines of history.

Reminding me that words can be good
Friends as well as the worst of enemies,
But good or bad, they are necessary
To the heart of the matter.

What would the sound that filters in
Your ear do without words?
Sound would terrify you to no end.
It would swirl in your ear howling
Without direction, images would bounce
Like aroma in the marrow of your bones.

There would be no light, only glare.
Your feet would not be feet, and your
Breathe would be only a smell that
Would curl like smoke and evaporate
into the air, leaving no clue of where the
Coffee is, making your taste buds
furious in your gums.

Words are a blessing from heaven; a
Swirl of vision; a milky way halo
                    Around your head.

Siesta With A Consonant

The thoughts of my teeth
Move my lips without effort;
Absent minded and safely
I sigh within. I am myself.
Though no one sees me,
And I dance nakedly like a
Wave over the horizon.

Yet I am afraid of myself,
Such a pity. I am afraid of
Distance, but nonetheless
I travel in full bravado
Through the universe.
Unfortunately, it is the mask
I wear.

Instead, I wish I were a
Clam and could noiselessly
Exist in a vacuum, where
Time does not matter and
Life would be marked by a
Seaweed
          drying in the sun

Soma Electric Vision

Soma how you have escaped me;
Writhing invisibly in a Valley of tears,
Tearing at my skin, my eyes, my palms
In an anomaly of impressions, making
My mind unsure if the vowel called I
Is just a myth.
Soma how you rumble like a
Mysterious wind without a howl, yet
roaring with an urgent need to find
your moment in Space...
          And in a cavity called Soul.

    Soma, your incessant need to find
Expression terrorizes me, and delights Me:
I am only a molecular cluster of sound
Wandering in a blind... or a star, a kin
To space who seeks homeostasis in
The electric magic of the universe

                    To Danny Castro,
                    a voice from the past

Journey 58

The Nith like water will find its way.It will seep through the marrow.
The long trek of violence must end, and humankind must come to
Grips with its destiny. Its relationship to the tules, the trees,
The rivers, (the Merced), which greens to Cressey and, the Mariposa
That created a marsh called Red Top, El Nido, Gustine and
Los Banos, Unable to crawl into the San Joaquin.

And, not to forget the lush beauty of a neighborhood known as the
Northside of the tracks, where the the children of 1940,
(World WarII babies), shrilled with innocence on the Le Conte
School playground, echoing those of the nearby Fremont School,
Where the big kids went.

Where now a parking lot and a slab called the county building hover,
And whose concrete and asphalt broke a tree line that once led
Where John Muir serenely nested, just on the other side of the Santa
Fe Line, a short distance from where the town ended.

So as time scrolls, the Nith of that memory, along with that of the
Mighty Galen Clark, which produced Lloyd Winston, Frank
Duran, Bobby Gutierrez, Bobby Shadrick, Johnny Smith, Hilder
Darrington, and Ralph Avila, whose vibrancy merged with the other
World War11 babies of the town...
And brought a Yosemite League Championship home to a place
Called Merced; a place that Tom Peck said showed no mercy, as he
Ate cold peaches on a hot day, along a Creek called the Bear.

It has been a journey, and we must rejoice. The class of 58 was a
Symbol of hope and, an inspiration to many of us / A needle sitting
High in the middle of our skulls...
        A Nith needed to nimbly walk in a universe called time.

Walking Tentatively

Struggling with my yawn, an ant crawls
Slowly beneath my feet, following another.
Its sturdy legs climb over a wet rotted twig.
I would smash it if it were summer and,
if the twig was dry; both would crackle
under my foot, but it is spring and it has
rained, and the ground is damp. The blade
of grass it carries is bright, beaming green
against its red spindled body. I Wonder if it
will turn black in the summer, and if it will
survive til then.

Wrinkles crease my face; I do push ups
daily, yet they remain. Will someone smash
me someday when my walk is slow? I
struggle with my yawn, watching an ashen
cloud overhead, and think of its wet breeze
pushing it, grazing my face.

The ant has reached its destination,
crawling under a rose bush, joining others
that are nibbling on a petal, dropping
The blade of grass neatly beside it. We are
both on a mission. Mine is to yawn.
Carefully, I walk over a puddle left by
The cloud, hoping that its shadow doesn't
crush me.

My Doctor

I have had the fortune to sing,
to eat green vegetables,
and to walk in a waken slumber.
thinking of witchcraft and of my
doctor who wishes to be a
bricklayer, and that complains
to the unjust human God.

My lips like lost kisses, eat
dirt looking for love.
The chatter of the morning
frightens me; its voices
drowned by the necessity for
money consume me.

I would like to strip bare of my
body. I do not need it anymore;
it has become a nightmare,
buying it shoes and hand made
socks from France.

I live in fear and apprehension,
(schizophrenia seizes me at the
hands), and my doctor only tells
me, to not drink booze
                    anymore...
And to learn to breathe like a fish.

Dedicated to Doctor Stuart

The Parody of Names

I speak to my friends, the Jorges, but that are called
George. I wonder if the gorge between the names
confuses them; I know it confuses me; I see George in
happy face configurations, but Jorge has a fullness
to it that swells the lungs, as both friends are
        alive with
vision, imbued with power in their hands that grip the
reality of life and, whose palms are grooved with lines
of determined vision.
                        Yet they are extremely shy.
Though...
            They speak their minds to the passing winds;
seeking the most quiet logic that only migrating birds
can hear, for people are afraid of them, and thus both
hide in webs of isolation to not disrespect the frail
souls that co-inhabit the earth with them.
I wonder how they would like to be best known
        or does
it really matter, as they mostly stare at their hands...
                Waiting for their guise to form in
quiet grace, waiting for their mother to call their
        name,
                    "Mi hijo ven acqui."

            Para mis cuates: Garcia y Verdugo

After My Vacation

In the deep, a tunnel inhales its wind drift.
The quiet air streams and, the eyes flutter
In the rays of the sun, nothing exists,
But a vapor of silence. A body requires
only the basics, so pure air can feast on
the earth's elements: crystals of light and
horizons with distant beaches that gleam
with
                    panoramas of
blooming skies, where the dark moaning
of the past expires, and where birds spread
their wings, opening new horizons of
                              hope.
The deep tunnel inhales the odor of a
nearby rose; quietly, asking the mirrors of
eternity... to settle a world whose body is
Poisoned by the language of crime.

To Diana Martinez' Neighbors, the Flying
Stocks

Spanish and Italian Only, Please

Vowels struggle in their effort to be heard; I would
Feel compassion for them, were it not they can be
Annoying shrills of discontent, their pitch becoming
Like children still unable to speak, or like parrots
In the jungle traumatizing silence, making the trees
Shutter.

The A and the U are easier felt, especially in Italian
And Spanish, but the E, I, and O are like shrieks
Of flickering lights that are quickly muffled by darken
Dust storms that sweep the skies.

How can three vowels in an alphabet of twenty-
Six letters, and in some languages more, have
The ability to dim the process of a mind's
Perception, leaving one in deft despair.

An image needs all its vowels, spaced out in a
Yawn, so that their echo can gargle in the fluids
Of the ear's cilia, and images can reflect in the
Mirrors of the Skull, and your thoughts like
Glittering Gold Fish can swim...
In the emotion of time, and eternity can become
A moment of grace where the reflection of your
Hands...
                Can glow.

Invisible Time

I move in a vibration of time.
Its vibrancy gnaws at me, as
decibels ask who are you, what
are you / while I sleep, soundless
thoughts clash then scatter and,
not finding a logical answer...
reject all the images that
the mirrors of my mind create
opening and closing in fluttered
silence.

You are but an incense of
Smoke that never evaporates
And, that hides under your
fingernails, so that you will not
Touch it; you are but
A memory: a memory that only
your mantra can intercept before
It slips into your blood stream,
So that your eyes can sleep.

You are a dream maker that
haunts you at night, so that the
Mirrors of your soul can rest.
As there is no one behind that
door, but a gnawing need for
words that will refresh the portals
Of your eyes, so that your
Thoughts can see while you
struggle through your
Stone Age needs.

Rudy's Night Club and The Ice Man

Where the identity swirls in dreams impossible.
And the me, the him, the she and, the he, evaporate,
hissing like dry ice, meandering in heavenly pursuit
of the real and the unreal...Not knowing that the
murmur of light, a close relative of the dark is searching
for a consonance with the us, a consummate of the
we, looking for harmony, as a saxophone searches for
Lungs with harmonic wings.

The identity, a tragic notion, saunters, looking for
notoriety, fame, for a place in civilization that will never
be because it lacks the snare of a benevolent drum,
the fingers of a maestro guitarist, or a pianist, progenies
from the Italian renaissance... To chord the soul from
its cove, so the He and the I will not struggle with the
Me and the She, in ways detrimental to the soul and,
surrender to words...

Words written with sharpened quills, meant to inoculate
and scuttle: alienating the struggles of fathers, sisters,
daughters and mothers, who along with brothers stir
in the memories of the Ice Man, El Hielero, Rudy
Merino's father; as his cart crawled from Childs to Fifteenth,
and from G to R in a sun that beat down on the town
and its Barrio dwellers, separated by the Southern Pacific
tracks... until they submitted to the quills of violence,
terrorizing the mind into conformity...

Alienating communities, driving wedges of death;
Poisoning human hearts, infusing them with rage and
hate; torturing people with thoughts of grandeur,
opulence and, deft demeaning vanities; robbing them
of La Lengua del Arte, The Language of Arte; a parlance
that is common to the all; an utterance that reaches
inwardly; coalescing the body with the pulse and its vibration,
melding into the marrow of the bone, cutting through
the curses of the past, and bringing charity to the soul
To a town that showed no mercy, as poetry and music
Ferments the air at Rudy's on Seventeenth.

Don Jose Merino was Merced's
First Latino City Councilmen

Rudy Merino

Lost... in a grandeur of words,
of peopled emotions, of time,
of friendships: Bobby Quagila,
Vernon Woods, of conflicts that
should have never happened,
of a space that as a result of an
I became a me.

A staunch believer of nothing
and everything, gullible to
nature, dreams and, to the ether
of a blooming flower
            in the shade,
delighting in the brightness of
day, waiting for the blues,
            Rudy's Blues;
a sound becoming younger in
The peal of light, in the rotation
of unseen consonants and,
in the echos of far
            away constellations.

His drum strokes, a vibration
from the palms, a sigh, a prayer,
a reflection of himself, but
more so: of a smile that
vibrates in sound, transcending
in the night, an opulent echo,
Whose Blue's beat
        Crescendos in the stars.

To Cindy Merino

Nothing

The weight of silence slithers; a raw
Writhing follows... by a crunching
Sound of bone; yet all is quiet.
An overcast sky breaking with sunlight
Glares; a moment has passed, but yet
The stillness of yesterday remains
Puzzled by unattended memories.
I do not travel in pronouns anymore.
It is hard to live in space with them,
yet, the blood flows: determined
and bold, surging forward, knowing
and not knowing, yet in its flush a
Universe sighs.
There is nothing more; human greed
Has destroyed the amoeba's hope
For a good breath; the heavens roam
above, beneath and around it......
Its eyes glimmer into the grey, blue
And white that permeates the sky.
One last sip of coffee: silence is a
          Blessing, why is there despair.

Happy Birthday World

The tyranny of the I; a sound that flounders within me; a
Creature that stumbled from the sea; a pulse of anger, a
Pulse of rage, that desires to be free & delight in a dignity
That was torched by a civility, where knights and nobles
Bend their knees, honoring their kings of be, calling them
Their holy seas, and whose guns and powder kegs went
Mad, wrecking customs for their Greed, and conquering
Sadistically, slaying natives for their needs, destroying all
Their senses shamelessly...
And, now I blindly strive in space and wind, to hear and
see my history, which wants to trace my roots of be to
their basic reverie and their desire to be free, so to
Rhyme my thoughts with care and to move beyond despair.
Understanding that I am, but an inhaling diaphragm,
Pressing for the purest air, to remove that cruelty which
Destroyed my liberty, and assist in the human task of
Breathing slowly in one's mask, for singing is our only task;
So that the lungs can come to rest and, the pelvis can
Secrete warm euphoria to our feet so to walk upon this
Turf with the blessings of the Earth.

Boleros in the Midst

Pitch a stitch in which a peach
tree grows; along the banks of
sandy foam; a rainbow blares from
above the rim as / heaven hums in
cogent sounds of sweet smells of
long ago and Lazy notes from a
sonnet's sob.
A fearful echo from the sky that
trembles deeply in my sight, blaring
Loudly as I sigh.
A fickle tickle far and wide; a
pulsation in the air; seeing bodies in
despair with cloaked faces every-
where; wrecking havoc on the word,
As politicians on the tear, destroy
The fabric and the care of
humanity's in sprit, giving those with
woeful charm: a chance to harm and
Cheat... with lying menacing deceit.
The empty bolero in me hums
With no perception of its thrum. I
think of the travesty of time whose
claw tears deeply in my spine,
Dredging fluids from the abyss,
Making humans lose their bliss, and
Now I wonder as I live / if happiness
Can still exist, and to my children
I compel to search for heaven in
                Their hell...
And make bolero wale loud, so
They can reach up to the clouds,
And find boleros in their stare: to sigh
With joy and peace of mind: in words
That float down from the sky.

Joe & Manuel
The Merced Boys

   The present is motionless; light floods
my writing room, too many shadows to
attend to / far away the horizon laves my
back; its hush washes away, foamless
in my mind / the shadows want
                          to converse,
but I am afraid of shadows / they move
without sound and feel like a sieve against
my heart / I think of Manuel and
          Joe Beruman / they were quiet.

   I was afraid of them until they smiled, but
their faces went quiet afterwards, and the
fear would reappear.

   Maybe it was the death of their brother
in the great war (that was not so great to
many), that affected them/ or perhaps
just the sorrow of their parent's loss that
weighed on them/they were an anomaly
within themselves / the neighborhood
was loud.

   They peddled bikes in the outstretched
grasslands that bordered their house /
making trails for the rest of us / they were
a fixture on 15th & R/no one will forget
them/they are like shadows..., complicated
in the motion of time / but friends to
               all who enjoy quiet /

A Nith of Silence

The nith of existence, what is that,
I ran into the word, while reading
a book called Vocal Wisdom; the
word has shocked me ever since,
leaving a denuded writhing,
defenseless to the sun light that hides
between the pages of other books
I read in discomfort and fear.

When darkness falls, I feel better:
its shadows seem to blanket me from
the incessant impulse that the word's
clarity demands; its vibration always
seem to be on fire, and tap water is
the only cure, as my fiery glands
thirst for taste and smell before the
ear can hear its call... while my body
hovers in wait for my cerebral to
find solace.

It is difficult, a difficult proposition.
Especially for those of us that are
encouraged not to see and hear,
the conquered; and each night when
Its din vibrates and the shadow cover
of darkness protects me.
I rejoice, as the nith needle, like
A Verdugo knife pierces clean,
and my skull can sing the megahertz of
my soul and, like a moth I float
from curtain to curtain in yet unheard
sounds of beauty and silence.

to the poets of the world

Fifteen Ways to Live or Die

Words: The mental heaven of the glands.
Glands: The flavored echo of words.
Words: The visual delight of thought.
Thought: The impressions of life.
Life: The echo of the heart beat.
Echo: The sensation of sound and light.
Sensation: The odor that touches your nose.
Nose: The organ that brings flavor to your taste.
Taste: The aromatic smell that touches your palate.
Touch: The shock of space after being born.
Space: The sky touching the sea that nourishes the land.
Land: The soil that grows food.
Food: Nourishment required body needs.
Greed: The obliteration of the human soul.
Benevolence: Humanity's hope for a buoyant existence.

Real Thought

Lingering in my past, I think of the
Girl with the dancing eyes; seized by
By a fazed memory, I know its only
A dream, as is all of life: Only
When one dies does one live, and
That is in the mind of those that
                    Loved you or didn't.
Life is funny in that way and,
Emotions nibble at you in doubt,
But in glorious delight: a power
Graced in you by the sun: the
Meaning of a daring moment &
the pulse that makes you human,
as you
        Watch time melt in your hands.

Finite Expression

A yawn should negate verse,
Removing the rhyme, the
                    meter
The cadence, and even the
idea and word; until only
the poem is left, and the
glow of its image explodes into
A consonant of sound where
its vowel
Becomes a mirage
and, the vapor of its echo, the
Conducting hand that
Make
            A sad world sing.

dedicated to Jorge Verdugo

Autumn Song, S. 400
Bountiful, Utah

A secret moment, an image without light, dark
but Illuminating, explosive in the heart
of the skull. Its radiant flash, a glare of sound,
satiates your soul with exuberance/you
breathe to the wonder of God, and the Universe.
And, captured by the echos of those thoughts,
you ruminate in the marrow of your bones, and
decide to walk down S. 400 to ponder. The
smell of the cool Autumn breeze touches your
palms, filtering to your feet, and body.
A symphony of sound, inhales, and a gourmet of
melodies serenade you; in awe, you want to
remember the moment, but it slips Into eternity
quickly, and hope someone hears it; it would
be a shame not to; the trees sway shedding
leaves, and the lawns glitter.

To the Slew

The Bishop, South 400

A leaf floating in the wind, a quiet wind;
Almost mute and soundless, but its
Chill touches my arms. and my body
snuggles against itself watching the leaf
Land, fluttering, before it settles on a
Grass recently sprinkled by rain.
A dark gleamed mahogany casket sits,
waiting to be lowered, as the space of
time hovers over those grouped, watching
it; a man, Curt Stock, known
As The Bishop speaks/   /His words
Are lost in the wind, and to the group
Whose faces are tortured with sorrow. The
man knows this, but He is a gifted Speaker
and speaks eloquently about The person in
the casket, Carlos Martinez, A Man that
taught him great humility, And restored his
faith in the art of human Love. He traveled
a great distance to
be with the grieving group that feels
the same way he does, and to speak his
heart's soul to the teared faces and, to the
wind, reminding them that a Great Human
has just past on to eternity, and that
He is in a good place with God, as the leaf
Scuttles near his feet, quivering.

To my friend, Curt Stock 3-4-22

Thought and Sense

To caress thought as it emerges
from the depth of silence and,
feel it simmer in a foggy mist,
emerging, struggling... waiting
for the teeth to nurture it, to
flavor it and wake it from the
whirl winds of emptiness, as
its gums, soak in desperation,
drowning in the dark waters of
history and, not allowed to
bask in a space called time,
where it can mirror among
the stars, meander & float like
a feather, becoming a breeze
and bathing in the ocean,
listening to its waves...
away from the uncivilized war
powers who claim they are
civilized / crashing
           the nobility of its taste.

Quiet

An
Expression
Ruminating
Alone /
Dispersing
An
Act
of divinity/
A
Lung
Lush in
Thought,
Seeking
Grace

A Feather of Hope

      To be in breath, to be in sound
To be in silence is profound.

A wave magnetic to be found in
nature's settings of our glare,
Fomenting visions with much flare.

Oh, hope of heaven and beyond,
A smell of flowers in our stare as
Light and wind caress the hair.

And internal silence comes to bare,
As quiet harmonies spark the air

With pungent mysteries and rays of
Dare with mirrors flashing everywhere

While mellow music strikes the ear,
Soothing people from their fear.

A Moment to Dance

Beautiful words fondle the impressions
that slide and fall on the pastures of
life; the pupils wait for the cornea
to breathe, to visualize them, but your
thoughts are not trained for that; they
move quickly as it is their nature to
flee, which is what they've been taught
to do, as they have been taken from
you...
You gaze at the stars; they are faraway.
You build mounds and pyramids to see
them, to touch them, and to dance
to the rhythm of their movements,
now you are stationary; you live in a
reservation, a dry piece of earth / far
from the forest that bred you and, you
dream of the streams that gave you life,
and wake to reality: the eyes must
breathe and, your words must illumine
the inner
       Hollows of your Heart.

A Murmur of Love

A word cannot live in space;
Yet it is too heavy to sink to the
Bottom of the sea.
A word like a stream must flow,
Wait for a sail to stir it, to flutter,
And to swirl it, so, it can skirl
and evaporate in your
Mind, fermenting in your inner,
Ear, spine, and uvula, making
it a wavering current of time:
eternal to those that visualize,
and inhale in it, as in a breath
called Jorge...
A metaphor, a shining blade in
The early sun, fearless in its
Gleam, skirling in his bones,
and vertebrae: a man, whose words
are his children... murmuring in his
Veins.

To Jorge, the Blade, Verdugo,
&
Jorge, the gracious, Garcia.

Memory

In my nothingness...
The heart beats like wings
In a cloudless sky /
My sentiments vanish,
And I am left without
Pain nor love, and my
Pores stare blankly
At the sky...
    I wonder what is
Going to happen to me
When my blood no
Longer seeks oxygen /
    Will I still love you...

Beyond The Me

The Indigenous continents where the
Sun and leafy glades colored the skin, And
the zero Point field of electromagnetic
Mediated awareness and hope: a
Place where the garden of eden was in
Bloom and the Human senses struggled To
capture time and the full essence of
A breath, and/ where the pupil gazed into
The Gravity of Space, and its eye
Moved horizons, creating the miracles
Needed to save a world from human
Blindness and Greed and/ the paradigms Of
class did not exist.

An Earth where vegetation refreshed the
Diminishing C0/2, and the sigh of the
lungs merged with a body's harmony and
The zero Point balance of Photons and
Sounds filtered in people's cells,
Quiet & Serene, giving them harmony of a
See.

A harmony incited by the flicker of the eye
and Zero Point Field of
                            electro-magnetic
Mediation and meditation existed; freeing
The Pelvis to its yawn... from thoughts,
Unterrorized by fears of civilization's
autocratic fields, and fictitious personalities;
of me, me, and celebrities bigger than
me began,
Nipping
At its root, soiling its awareness of time,
ruthlessly attacking its human way
Annihilating the zero Point of he, an old
Indigenous way to Be, before the
Invention of the wheel when
Walking healed the fifteen second mind's
Decree, and Heart decease did not exist.

The Lorenzo, Merced Poem in Prose

The best of the Gavacho, Larry Anderson, Ronnie Hall, Tommy Bass, and Henry Fuzzy Broughton were the best. There were others, Paul Brown, the Baldwin brothers, Delmar Laffon, Billy Shirts, Lloyd Hill and the Farmer brothers. It was an interesting time; all of us in the neighborhood living barely above poverty, but many of us living considerably below it. When we spoke, it was mostly with empty stomachs, so our words had be loud to suppress our hunger. We thought that if we talked loud and fast enough that our bodies would be stimulated to keep on going. Going where, we did not know, but we were told that there was an American Dream waiting for us, and so we struggled believing that there was a Sharon Douglas waiting for us. Her father Ray owned the Pine Cone by the Train Station, and one near the post office.

A girl whose father's riches was going to see us through, and so we went to the movies, and became involved with fast cars or fancy stock ones that we turned into our own image. It was an innocent feast of the senses raging in a world of supposed plenty; a world where some of us became infested with liquor, drugs and violence: searching for the dream.

Our bodies finally gave, and we thought, What the Fuck? Some of us now have many children and grandchildren, some of us with ruined penises only produced what it wanted to produce, and now there are only a few of us. But we were Brave men. Perseverance was the key, and we strutted until like old stallions, had to be sent to pasture to see the sun... set and rise.

We remember old songs, and our hearts heave, some of us would like to do it again, and some of us say that those eighty odd years were enough. But the sunsets are nice and the dawns even better, as we wake to another day. Grateful that we are still here, listening to our breaths, and to the laughter of our descendants, sharing in their hardships, and wondering if they will be tenacious like us.

A Chichimeca in Search of his World

Invisible Man, Yo

I am the
invisible man.
My Yellow shirt
With blue
        lines
and
        Brown
Gold spots
blend into
the concrete
Green of
  of the huge
library.

A fan buzzes
  noisily; the
sockets of the
eyes
      bulge
    tired red:
Ben Franklin,
John Hancock
    and the
Constitution
signers
  stare at me
vacantly.

Their fat bellies
and stiff
        Knees
make my blood
run
without oxygen.

The colors...
The colors
      of those
sounds
      scream
in my
        veins,

and gargles
of destroyed
children scratch
at my throat.

I A.............M
        I am
the Invisible Yo
in love with
a green-eyed
Cuban,
a Boricua with
the skin of
shining leather
and
    the smell
of pine trees
in the early
                dusk.
I am
        In love
    with America
South, Central
and North,
                with
Its people
                formed
by the sun
and the
                tropics
whose sweat
and color
        make the
air dance with
melancholias
        of past
Horizons
and
        Dawns,
of Machu Picchu,
of Mayan grandeurs,
and of Aztecean &
        Chichimeca
Determination.

I am
the invisible
        tired
of being a
      stranger with
with his
        Time.

Mysterious Existence

I am awake, but my eye lids sag.
I sit paralyzed, dozing at my writing desk
frustrated / unable to see, unable to sing,
and unable to cry. My thoughts need
clarity; they want to speak, and /though
I speak an array of languages, I can't
seem to settle on any. The constant
present has a grip on them and it wants
to compress every fiber of their soul into
a nothingness of breath; yet the thoughts
crave pictures and words, but mostly
they prefer motion: the perfect golf swing,
the perfect yawn, and the perfect vibration.
    As a result my thoughts wander
mindless mysterious; riddled with bullet
holes, lacking perception, and not caring
if they are dead or alive in fear of the
constant present: reaching out in
desperation to tonic salesmen who promise
them everything, but who only want their
skin to conceal themselves in.
    You are a seed, A slight flutter of the
eye lid echos / to settle the commotion in
your thoughts; you are a particle, a wave,
and, an entity that must never lose sight
and understand that what the tonic
Salesmen are selling is not the answer.
    You should not fear your thoughts,
They are not alien beings. Your thoughts
are messengers of your vibrations telling
you that you need language to breathe,
to hear, and to see the moment that
evolves in you and, to understand that you
are free, that here is no past nor future /
that you are just diaphragm needing a
vowel...
    A consonant floating in a space you
call self that you created, and that has
Created you / A memory that will live
                into eternity, gyrating...

Notion Impaired

A notion, an image, a shadow
After a storm, a clear blue note
of sky hovering like a symphony
over the land; a splurge of
orange flowers dash the landscape,
and the purple Lillies flourish
In the deep green meadows of
spring, as antelope, elk, and deer
Meandered near, grazing.

I think of the Yokut looking for
seeds, acorns and tule clubs to feed
their children, singing hymns to
their elders, and rejoicing in the
abundance of life and land.

The fish splashing in the
River Merced, big sister to the
Chowchilla and the Mariposa that
never reach the San Joaquin,
but that nourish Sandy Mush,
El Nido and Red Top, but which are
are now destroyed by the old
World's greed, razing its land,
and replacing nature's way that
was sacred to its natives

Y Haci Fue

And that is how it came
to be... the sound of the consonant
Like a hammer without a handle,
Tearing the soul of the impression
Into an agony without foam,
Destroying the flow of the sigh
Like a glass shredded by wind.
As the alien pain, full of greedy
Gods, whose teeth, like lances
Plunged into her belly, her intestines,
And into her heart's inner door,
Relentless until...

There was nothing but a barren
Landscape where people went
Looking for the promised that
Never came, and her humanity
Withered in the dirt, as the
Lances exploded into a crazed
Whiteness, and the cries of the
People were muffled, like vowels
In a frozen scream.

Orona's Lament

The Mexican
The middle Mexican
The Mexican in the middle
The smell of turpentine
Casts dry
Shadows
Over the Valley Floor
In its drift
Hues of old Zoot-Suits
Wearing high heels
Waver in the sun
Bleeding in perspiration
As ants
Stumble
In the dust
carrying their prey

La Llorona has
Discovered Elvis Presley
And
Chicanos speaking
In tongues huddle
Around telephone poles
Dancing to his beat
While toothless Cholo
Children
Bite at their bellies
Their abdomen looking
For their gums
saying Hey Y'all

Magnetic Hope

Fiery thoughts hew deep
in my veins, heaving,
flaring like hot lava in me;
my mind, a surrogate
of my brain, dawdles
in wait, cleaved by the
fury of a visual cortex who
is in a fiery battle with
an imagined self, waiting
for a blood flow that
seeks the silence it needs
to renew Its connection
to the cosmos, and allow
the heart to engage the
lungs to cool a brain that is
constantly in fire and, in
search of words with
magnetic magnificence
        to douse its flame.

Human Drought

Lilacs and roses in a garden growth of odors, inhaling organs. The clouds high up in the sky, and an autumn breeze in a cool spring day; all is clear; the body breathes and the skin opens its pours ...widely to the sky...

I am nature. Where did I go wrong? Did the mysteries outside the womb terrify me, or did my predecessors' wounds leave haunting aromas in the air?

Seething nights hover over the mountain valleys now (the lilac oder absent in the simmering heat), and the farmers weep, choking, feral in their cry, not for herding the natives off their lands, but because they need water for their vast vegetable crops, vineyards and, almond orchards (water that the land's ancestors watched with care), honoring it with flutes of grass, and rattles sacred to their heart.

Water that was drunkenly soused in the name of manifest destiny, profits, land schemes, and greatness: giving the chosen ones license to dry up Tulare Lake, leaving the native in drab sorrow.

The Ghost Dance was outlawed and, the joyous ebullience of the land was left ladened with silt, and its people muffled, unable to breathe, as the christian god suffocated them (the anglo bribing them with young boys and girls and heresies of gold).

That shinning metal that crushed the intestines of natives and their souls, lacerating the veins to their hearts, leaving them crippled, gasping for their lungs; as now they scroll for Crow, Hawk and Coyote in paved parking lots and shopping centers: (muted, without vowels and consonants), their intestines cloaked in liquor.

Though, that is not the issue. The earth, dry with clods, parched... Its surface land sinking... as pumps dig deep into its belly and tractor plows carve dust that sails in the wind.

The tongueless land is thirsty and arid, unable to give birth, but do not blame the farmer. He is an endangered specie / your keeper / His god is greed, an organ-less fist.

Dedicated to Buffalo Ochoa

Dios Mio

The language of the Bible
assault my senses and
like a drunk, my perceptions
stagger in soundless echos,
not allowing the veins to
murmur to the harmony of
their flow, leaving me
powerless to the the pull of gravity.
in desperation I seek vowels
and consonants to settle
a wandering mind whose
body has been stolen by history.

I think of the Virgin Mary, and
of the passion I feel for women.
Their bodies, their flesh, the
softness of their skin when I
imagine touching it, and my
hands become heavy with sin.

The turmoil and torture that
follows are unbearable, so I try
to hide them, only to stuff
them in my crotch where desire
and passion become a muffled
agony of silence, and my sky
becomes a haze; it's breeze turns
into a gust that swishes like
a blade in a yearning ire.

The language of the Bible has

hurled me into a purgatory of
confusion, my need to fly
among the bird's shadows:
unable to touch their feathers,
unable to float in the wind with
them, as my words need
permission to think, and...

My breath has become a mist,
foamless to the spume of my
thoughts that gasps in the sins
of The Bible: becoming daggers
in my heart that muffle the echos
of my throes, and perceptions
of a world filled with love and
essence.

Empty Hands

The drip of rain splashes, and the drops
of water gleam in an overcast sky.
The magic of the moment is wet, and a
hesitant silence falls over the Valley
Floor, as the roar of incoming clouds
thunder from beyond the coastal range,
in the distant Pacific; their crescendos
brighten the dark clouds, then fade into
rumbling roars.

The land is thirsty, and dry mosses form
on the ferns, and on the slopes of the
foothills, once home to hunter gatherers
who roamed seeking nutrients and spirts
from the sounds of nature, but they are
no more, there are only casinos, as cattle
graze and cars zoom, going to Yosemite,
the promised land of the Awhahneechi.

A Madness not in Vain
Paseo Artistico

The dispersing of sound; the smell, lemon blue, soothing like the scent of a tree blossom stirring in the oder of my heart; undernourished, I float in a wavering day, clouds mist in sun and dew, and I Inhale trying to decipher its aroma / but its wayward matter dissipates in horizons that fume in the bones of time.

My ancestors look at me from their inner souls in askance. Did they do the right thing, did their determination to love you, and to nourish you, no matter what, paralyze your senses of be? The echo of the question makes you gasp in confusion. A needle burns in your sternum, and...

You seethe, looking for clarity, but there is none, and your feet feel lost in the hum of the moment, as anxiety straddles your soul, and you do the best to keep your balance, and unfettered, you look for the gyration and cadence that you inherited from your Ante-Pasados, and float In the past and present, walking tentatively up Twenty-Fourth Street from Bryant to the El Tecolote venue, where celebrated Mission Latino organizers will discuss their lives in struggle.

Smells of sauces, quesadillas, tacos, pan dulce, along with stands of assorted fruit greet you from its walkways arousing the tropical fragrance in you. And not to stumble you squeeze the palm of your beloved to find the softness of harmony, and the mystery that captured you; the woman that your mother choose for you, whose mole and rice decorate the passing winds of history, as your mother's ancestors ordained.

You walk in the heart of San Francisco's Mission District, mesmerized by its its Latino festiveness, as youth: CAPOEIRA and MDYMP express their artistic valence and heritage of song and dance to a gathered crowd of aficionados, followed by Enrique Ramirez, the famed Mission Musician / who after speaking briefly to you / rushed off to emboss Paseo with his Los Peludos beat... Viva Caballo!

Your heart sways in the rhythmic oder of your be: Viva John Santos, Viva Santana, and long live los Artistas de la Mision who past and present expressed their art to the universe... with glory and joy, unfettered.

La Gente del Viento

Platico con una voz sin ojos,
cuyas palabras pierden su
fuerza en silabas incompletas,
Llevando en su alas, aullidos
deshechas por un viento
         nublado de corraje.
Un tubarron oscuro, vestido
    en blanco.

Somos y no somos...
         Chichimecas, vestidos
por un sol / enamorados con
el viento.

The People of the Wind

I speak to a voice without eyes,
whose words lose their vibrancy
in incomplete syllables.
                  Carrying... on
its wings, howls dispersed by
by a wind
         clouded in anger, by
A dark storm dressed in white.

Are we or are we not
         Chichimecas, coated
by a sun & enamored with the
wind.

The Sine Wave

A Sudden rejection of sound:
the shoulders tighten, the breath
halts at the throat (the front
of the spine), and molecules
die where the gums touch the
The teeth...

The flesh smolders in insulated
agony looking for its hands, feet
and eyes / against a quiet death.
I am alive and dead at the
same-time; however, my eye-
lids blink and my pupils flare.
The cornea needs to breathe and
carbon dioxide molecules
stream through its cells,
blending light; I inspire; my heart
breathes vowels / And my brain
reflects consonants.

Words are my salvation; their
Impressions are my soul.
Their smell of nectar is the aroma
between
Life and Death and... do not know
that I exist...

Dead and Alive, I venture not
recognizing which, but a wisp of air
enters my pores, and the
worm that hardened into a spinal
cord smiles: a yawn glows like an
invisible neon in my hands and
feet, as Conga beats of nature
erupt.

Lets Dance

    Transcendent voice, echo of silence,
how you steal through the pitch of
darkness, creating Light, with the motion
of the stars.

    Your vision has not left me; though
I utter it in other tongues.
At times my throat croaks with moments
From its flowering past, and touching it
        I surge in leaping revery
Extolling nature in my soul, making
Rhapsodies of joy.

Your reveling timbre reverberates on
the earth, as the sea breeze dances in
My feet, and in the fibers of my be.
I can see and breathe again,
        and new dawns rouse in my
bones, while writing lyrics in the snow

Dedicated to the Chaushilas Yokuts

Alive & Well

Silent aromas caress the shadows of
my thoughts, and though strangers to me,
my pours inhale them. I peer at the
distance, horizons bloom, and glimmers
of light, scented with flowers appear.
      Their aromas spreading through a
soft breeze wrap around a grove of pines,
and bury themselves in my silent stare;
their scent, a marvel of life, waken
the smell of pungent green, as their
needles tumble to the ground, mixing
with leaves of oak, and eucalyptus
that stand near, sharing my enchanted day.
      A surge of life overwhelms me, and
The sweet tang of life wakens me...
Alive with the sparkle of smell, I bristle in
bliss and delight: knowing that nature will
never betray me, and that my eternity will
shine in the stars.

The Page

It is a way of being alive.
A slight surge of the hand
Following the line, blue,
Against a blank white
Page; filling it with cantos
Of resurrected memories.

It is the way I caressingly
Hold the pen, as if it
Were my mother's hand,
Warm between the index
and the thumb, but unable
To wrap the rest of my
Fingers around it.

I think of the tortured
Life she lived because
She was an Indian, beaten
By her Spanish husband.
Yet loving him because
He gave her children,
And so I write in pain for
Her; she loved me.

To My Mother, Guadalupe Gallardo

Hands

To hold an echo of sound
In a yawn, and feel its
Moment spread from your
Hands to eternity...
Where nothing exists but
the sparkle of the stars /
where the invisible bond
of human friendship is
the key to existence, as
Time sits empty in
space, and the roar of
farmworkers spread over
the land.

To the Memory
of Bear Creek Camp

Invisible Time

I move in a vibration of time.
Its vibrancy gnaws at me, as
decibels ask who are you, what
are you / while I sleep, soundless
thoughts clash then scatter and,
not finding a logical answer...
reject all the Images that
the mirrors of my mind create
opening and closing in fluttered
silence.

You are but an incense of
Smoke that never evaporates
And, that hides under your
fingernails, so that you will not
Touch it; you are but
A memory: a memory that only
your mantra can Intercept before
It slips into your blood stream,
So that your eyes can sleep.

You are a dream maker that
haunts you at night, so that the
Mirrors of your soul can rest.
As there is no one behind that
door, but a gnawing need for
words that will refresh the portals
Of your eyes, so that your
Thoughts can see while you
struggle through your Stone
Age needs.

Guadalupe

The memory of my mother cries into tears.
Their sorrow glisten, as they drop quietly
On the purple linen with yellow flowers that
She knitted; her umbra lacing into the design
Of the table I sit at surrounded by Machado
Borjes and Vallejo books.

For I have no other friends to console me,
As the space between the walls of my heart
Require consonance.

I ask my friends for strength, and they give
Me the soul of their subterranean hearts,
And their passion for love, the color blue,
And offer solace from their hidden
Chambers, and hope from their trampled
Lives...
Awake, breathing under the cover of their
pages.

Chano, my Son

As the dusk of
Autumn descends,
And my grey hair
Now thinning,
Scatterers, puffed,
Like cattails in
An eternal wind
without memory,
And the sound of
Motors racing in
The stars,
I ponder
Your essence,
And wonder if
The seasons, in
Their quiet
rotation will
Caress you with
The wisdom of
        Time,
Or if they will Tumble you into
An abyss of Shadows and
Dark constellations
Where mishap
And misfortune
Journey...like
Blind lovers,
    In a Tumultuous
        Sky.

To be human was to be White skinned, and American; the winds Blew winnowing through his dark brown hair; he was not as dark as his brother that was called el Negro by the older brothers Who were beige. He sat among them in gaps of breath, trying to Inhale their conversation. It was an unhappy group that had Become Mexican by default, as they were Chichimeca Guamare. He looked at el Negro, the brother he followed in succession, whose Dark eyes gleamed, shinning next to a fire that roared Hot Blues, Reds and Purples, while their hunched Bodies leaned forward to see If the heat of the flames would warm the blood that flowed within, But that only touched patches of their hands and faces, but Never the feet.

They huddled around the flames, cursing their existence, blaming God for a merciless cold wind that slapped at their faces, and that Had brought a rain, flooding the field crops that sat between the Mountain ranges, making work scarce, and supplying them only with Canela, Cinnamon Tea, and Pilonsio, a hardened rock candy Shaped in a cone, as scarcity loomed in the Valley, fed by an over Supply of Braceros Workers that had brought the field wages down, While the vegetables the family harvested, along with most of the Meat the vaqueros tended on the hillsides was sent overseas, for a War to save America and the World from Fascism and Communism.

Their Mother, a Mestiza the color of leather, a small Indian Woman, with curly black hair and the rounded features of an African Princess watched over the group, praying and telling God that her Sons did not mean what they said, and to forgive them for cussing At him, that she would say a rosary for their sins to him.

The boy sat dumbfounded, among the vibrations of the voices, And body gestures, rubbing his hands before the wood stove that Lit the family tent, that clustered with others to form a labor camp that sat next to a huge barn, burnt black brown by the sun and a Winnowing wind, that the Cows and the Braceros shared at night... Each having their own stalls.

The boy looked at his mother, his only connection to Reality, and Clarity, in askance, as he listened to his neurons spark without images, And to the microbes in his body... without nutrition, unable to inhale What the sound of the words Gavacho and Americano meant, as the Color White was only visible in the boned ashes of the wood after the Life of the fire went out, while his mother's eyes, beseeching to the Heavens did not notice his plea.

Guamare, Chichimeca Prayer

Of nature's
flares and pungent airs, creating notions of much glare in the pitu-
itary without despair, where vowels can glisten with much dare,
shining fibers in the air where consonants can rhythmically
compare... life's movement in my hair, and notions can procure a
depth of eternal human flare, shining its luminosity on to me,
inspiring echos without care, so my nature can procure... depths of
fibers in my hair, and my ear can Learn to hear quiet whistles every
where, and vowels and consonant can create pungent auras in my
stare, and help my body rise... creating potions with much care, as
rhythmic motions come to bare and, make me think that I can dare /
to walk unfettered on the air.

   I should have never abandoned the study of German or for that
matter any other language that I may have sought refuge in, for
English and Spanish insult my senses and I grunt insanely in much
pain. My teeth grasping for spurts of sound, suffocating in strange
winds While panting longings in my ears for hopes of long melodic
Otomanguean Vowels interspersing with hard halting consonants of
the Guamare, whose arrows
tore through the steel nets of the Spanish, who not only stole the
Land, But the harmonic echo in my eye. Nonetheless, I am still the
same as the stars above that bestowed vision to my virgin brain /
remind me that nature still contains my soul in the gravitational
movement of the poles.

El Mojado

To writhe in the depth of silence
Where darkness becomes a pitch
Of light that only a vowel can see.
And its reverie becomes a song
That the heart can faintly hear,
as the moan of time reflects in the
glitter of our space...

Out stretched in the universe, I
roam; my feet pining to touch the
soft velvet of its space: meadows
forest and the trees, as my nature
deep inside presses tight against the
lungs, so my ears can sing and
prance in a note of revelry / to the
Honor of the Earth.

I want the universe to hear
that I am matter of its core; not
an alien nor illegal, but a kernel and
a seed of its substance and its
stead.

My people... with crafted hands
burned the dry grasses of its lands
to protect the forests and its woods.
Refreshing their meadows to rebirth,
and caressing them with care,
so that nature could thrive in spring.

My wind is the same as yours.
You are the salt water immigrant,
please be kind; your raging greed
has destroyed my essence, though
not its reverie and dreams.

In Wait

I color myself in blue; not because
I am sad. It is because in the blue
Of the night, the skies glisten in the
Darkness of thought with clear
vision; vaporizing the heart with
New ways to aspire, as descending
Songs of the eye fill the lungs with
Chimeras of forgotten oceans,
Its waves washing over the images
Of the day: busy shopping and
Looking for love where none exists,
Or hoping that the day can heal the
Wounds of humankind...
That is why I go to bed early, so to
Wait for the blue of the night, and
Wait for the arms of my deceased
Mother and,
Feel the hope of her warmth

Anxiety on Hold

Bewildered by the silence of time, the moment
disassembles itself, scattering fugaciously in
an ephemeral and evanescent wind of darkness
whose sweeping force leaves a wounded hollow
in the cavity of thought: a blindness and a
swelling in the pith of its heart: an anxiety
caused by anxieties whose currents
drift and quiver / undefined by weightless words
that flee in rapid tides, seeking clarity in the
waves of an ocean,
       Swaying in the glare of a roaring moon.

To my grand & great grandchildren

Empty Hands

The drip of rain splashes, and the drops
of water gleam in an overcast sky.
The magic of the moment is wet, and a
hesitant silence falls over the Valley
Floor, as the roar of incoming clouds
thunder from beyond the coastal range,
in the distant Pacific; their crescendos
brighten the dark clouds, then fade into
rumbling roars.

The land is thirsty, and dry mosses
form on the ferns, and on the slopes of
the foothills, once home to hunter
gatherers who roamed seeking nutrients
and spirts from the sounds of nature,
but they are no more, there are only
casinos, as cattle graze and cars zoom,
going to Yosemite, the promised land of
the Awhahneechi.

Chichimeca Yo

Seeking the center of my universe has been my quest.
I have mauled it through my eighty years of existence,
And never has a finite answer ever appeared and, now
Going on two years beyond that span, feel that perhaps
The search will last forever in the motion of my stir,
As it evokes a glancing light in my mind that never
Sleeps; a light that wavers like an eternal dance in the
Marrow of my bones, as its visions of harmony appear
In a resonance where talking is done in silence and/
Where the body remains suspended in a glare of
sound... And, life is but a memory of Fragments that
Behold me, giving me the perseverance to withstand
Gravities' onslaught, as I form my own black Hole in
Space / brimming with glee / as the faces of my
Descendants sparkle in flashing colors...

Chichimeca Yo.

To Fernando Hernandez, and his Pata Rajada friends

Palo Sagrado

The odor of palo sagrado, sanctified
wood, seeps into my nostrils/the
fingers that
hold it, tranquil and serene, rest
suspended in the air / all is quiet as the
inhaled aroma, like the touch of
a feather, descends from the middle of
the skull,
          to the spine,
                    waist, and finally
               Down to the feet and toes,

I am one with the horizon, as its scent
floods the prism of my soul with
floating visions and,
                    wavering images
of meadows and forgotten forests, as
          sauntering cars crawl about in
daylight / on roads that ripped the
          fragrance of my wooded past...

Enchanted, my dissipating throat
becomes an organ of my lung, and the
alien language does not tear
     nor violate the ethereal of my be.

As my stone age pulse seeks its
Verve
     in the rocks and gaze of long ago,
and the music of the flashing moon
says:
     Yo Chichimeca: with a glow...
          Seeing nature in its flow.

Some Where

To feel my yawn
spread its magnificence
To my soul, and for my
eyes to wander in an
eclipse of splendor/
touching the cavities
of my verve...
Looking for harmony
and grace in a world
        where the moon,
horizons and stars are
my kindred spirits;
knowing:
that without them, I
would be lost in space.

The Rooster Awakens

There, over there, where the flowers,
Where the exquisite lilies lie still,
Where there is no wind nor
                            blasphemies.
Where the sea never threatens,
There, there, where the quiet silence
Like a drowned rumor becomes a
Yawn, and your cavities with wide eyes
Inhale the movement of the stars.

There, there over there...
                            They walked
Barefoot, to not disturb the autumn
Flowers before the winter came.

To the Rooster and the Natives
of Ewell's Bar, Fresno, Cal

Canto en Flor

Is it a nibble; is it a doubt / or
Is it a nuance of life, the impressions,
And the glands that gush with gusto
In your pallet and mouth, opening
Your jaws to an urge called
Want... like an ocean seeking its
Shore, and your sailor eyes seeking
Horizons of grace that don't exist,
But to the imagination; the slow moving
Wind that stirs it, and wants you to
Relate to the reality of you who perhaps
Only exists because you carry your
Family's coat of arms, its history in
Your heart, and, the wonder of that yawn
Carves rivulets of thought
In your bones, and the stir of humanity
Furrows through your marrow / that
Silent wonder that hums in your teeth
Like a forgotten song, singing.

To Juan Domingues & Family

Human Instinct

    I live in fear of Language.
The space between a vowel
And a consonant screams
In a screech of silence that
wake my parasympathetic
Cells in delirium; it is a wonder,
that its echo has not
shattered my skull to pieces.

    My only defense to it has
Been to sing and yawn, and
At that, I do both badly...
It is a sin to yawn, and my
Ear is not trained to hear the
beauty in my soul...

    Yet I am addicted to its
din, its gentle breath murmurs
like a brook, streaming
Over pebbles in a morning sun.
And the waves of far away
ocean sounds that slither in
My bones are a wonder to me,

Yet, I choke before their echo.
How did I become a stranger
To my central nervous system
Whose fingers spread
Throughout me in a maze of
Neurons that are both friends
and enemies.

    How did the threads of
Time, and History
Make me afraid of the silence
Within, blinking in a wonder of
Fear and delight as I try to
Create a better world / or at
Least save myself from
            The one I live in.

To the Natives of the New World

Indigenous Thought

Recognizing my thoughts, echoing
In the variation of their vibrations,
And in the glow of light that walks
Behind them / casting curved
                Shadows at their feet.

Recognizing their eternal howls of
Mortification in the mystery of my
Situation / A tenor bestowed by
Deliberate manifestation, on the
Back of my established civilization.

A terror of time's depravation and
Hostile premeditation; forcing my
Mind into stilted obliteration, strafing
It with indignation; Though, doth it
gathers, in contemplation, moving
In a finite form of self preservation.

Casinos in the Midst

Silence, motion of time suspended.
How you seep like a stranger in my
Heart / how you caress my bones with
Your hovering breath, causing nightmares /
Many times I have tried to speak to
You, my friend, darkness without eyes,
But your stare, vacuous and sublime
Humbles me.
    And only my teeth and eyes have the
Courage to disturb you when they are
Hungry for food, and are startled by
the passing clouds for rain to soak the
Desert sands that I walk on, looking
For corn and vegetables.
    Why can you not speak to me more
Clearly; I want to see the Valleys and
Your Mountains, and Grazing Meadows,
Where animals roamed & without the fear
Of darkness of a now shattered soul.
        I do not want to die in a casino...
Sparkled and broke / with electronic
                Sounds ringing in my ears.

Manifest Destiny

Humankind Unraveled

I have unraveled my humanity
I am not a man, though of mankind.
My fingers of thought scroll the
Heavens, counting the stars, hoping
That eternity will be kind, and
	Allow me to finish my task.

Startled

My Breath startled by the nature
of life, and, the idea of a me,
Struggles with reality and non reality.
How could both be true to notes
Called A & G and to pitches called
High C, Alto or Soprano...
And unable to hear them, I ask
Am an I, a Be or an E, and how does
A body transform from pitches to
vowels, and how did
I become a me.

Confused, I lose myself in role play.
Am I a citizen, father, grandfather,
great grandfather, husband, or
brother, though, most of my siblings
have passed and my inherited
family diminished, I am afraid and
Not afraid, as I am one and no one.

But a doubt, invisibly to the mind
that seeks words to help the body
breathe, and to not stray and
coagulate and, allow the desperate
clashes of humanity and inhumanity
to creep in, and allow the vanities
of fear to destroy the uvula of
                    Life and Hope.

Betty's Place

When the motion of time awakens, and
my hands move slowly in the dark,
touching the contours of my bristled,
aging face and flesh and, the fingers
rubs the lashes of the eyes, waking my
blood from a from a fantastic dream,
where the River Merced flows through
a village crusted in a history of blacksmith
shops that repaired the wheels of heavy
wagons going to Snelling, Sonora, and
to the gold fields in Agua Fria;

Hopeton, the only settlement in a raw
Merced County to house a church,
perhaps two at that time; a place
called Forlorn Hope by miners who did
not find gold, and moved on; the banks
too high, unlike Hornitos and Quartsburg
whose contours slopped into rocky
beads of water that glittered; Hopeton,
a magic place that I like to visit, and
imagine its once bustling community
that instead grew fruit trees and almonds.

Hopeton, a place I like to stop by, and
buy a beer at its little store and, sip it
slowly as I watch the water flow near
where Front and Bradford Streets were,
cooling myself under its river oaks,
feeling its once bristling history, but that
Now is littered by overgrown grass:
where its descendants have to trample
over weeds, and discarded buildings
to find the cemeteries...
                    Where their loved ones lie.

To Betty Anderson & Family

Nature's Anomaly

Beneath the sleeping woods,
dreams and shadows meld;
everything is in full light, stars
gleam... a cricket chirps.

A refreshing breeze touches
the lips and magic eyes play
in the piety of love and, a pungent
scent of pine stabs the heart.

You know that my troubles
seek the quiet and the serene.
I come from solitary paths.

The night is sweet and relaxing,
a blue night of spring caresses
new flowers.

I have smiled in silence;
I have spoken to the heavens,
And the fog has brought me
Blessings from foreign lands.

I have slept among perfumed
meadows, whose grasses
dream of time; nonetheless,
in my spark-less eyes, sweet
tears tremble.

I see and speak, while the
violins mourn their sorrow: and
not to cry, I smile with amiable
indifference...
a cigarette burning ashes
                in my soul...

Jails of the Mind

The song in the eye is silent;
smothered by teeth that flavor for
food where there is none / as the
saliva strangles the uvula, the
yawn, not caring / not wanting
to smell nor taste; fearful of the
carbon dioxide needed
for its brain to hear: afraid of its
vibrations & bewildered by its
many voices that stare without
seeing.
As the mind sits against a
lamppost, an abandoned building,
or a littered
freeway underpass, surrounded
by magnificent homes
vegetating.
Unable
to penetrate a dark storm that
has settled in its midst, terrifying
the marrow of
its teeth with phantom sounds,
as they gnaw on meaningless
competitive and materialistic
Nouns and Pronouns
that mute the lungs into disuse,
igniting the mind to palpitate
quickly...
with no time to split the atom
of the imagination / which roams
scattered in the galaxies;
        unable
to perceive its particles, unable
to
hear them in its palms and brain/
where nature can teal rhythms
into it
so that its dopamine can chime
Symphonies from its peal.

Fear

Feral energy,
    Annoying rage.
Focal expression,
    Afflicted rot.
Flow emanating,
    Ardous ruin.
Fainthearted exertion,
    Agonized rose.
Faulty entrapment,
    Ascetic revolt, to
    All that is fruitful.
    Finite & fair.
Fragile foible,
    The Lingering
    Resonance of
    A consonant
    That refuses
    to become a
    Vowel.

Prism & Prison

    Before light reveals a word, and time
Descends on it, menacing it with urgent
Cries of relevance and irrelevance,
leaving it without decibels, mute in moaning
despondency.
Leaving it chaotically, unable to see nor to
Hear... Its palms pleading for a lucent
                    Touch of the hand.
Oh Word, thorn of salvation, Clock of
time!
    Why has man twisted you into grates of
Steel with spikes that plague the core
of your curiosity, piercing you with
      fissures, allowing you to flee sightless
Without the true mirrors of your
Reflections and fears, unable to become
whole and harmonic to the eternity of
the moment, and to the sleepless lungs
of the verve...

World Order

    I talk with you at a distance,
waiting for words to spur forth ionic rays,
bright with meadows, where colossal
bumble bees, orange
    in the sun, ferry among the trees,
as I speak in a foreign tongue, unimaginable
to man. My heart is a gargle, and I gasp like a
spastic, steadying my head, demurely on my
shoulders, hoping that my words to you go
uninterrupted, and that the sigh of my pulse
is not lost.

    Nonetheless, I feel like a mute,
helpless in a wisteria of thought (and jumbled
nuances). I have spoken to many, and
still the harvest of potatoes is low. There
is still war, and beings are suffering from an
identity crises; they are not who they
                         seem to be.

    Sí mamá, limbs are being torn from
people in the name of humanity. A hand
named David is getting revenge on the
populations, and my knees, elements of
bone, frail with love, suffer. The soft tissue
they are made of: are not for chasing stars.
They are made for walking, for feeling the
texture of earth move under them, and for
their toes to grip the dirt.

    I speak to you at a distance Mother,
from a universe, where the echo of tears tremble,
and where eternity is terrorized by time.
A device measured by numbers, where dignity
is allowed...
              only, if you count in silence.

Rage and Brutality

The silent hum of distance quietly threatens
My lungs, leaving patches of clouds, scattered in
The portals of my soul, and like a hollowed horizon,
Mountain Less, without trees and pasture, I blink.
Desperation seizes me and... tormented, my
Thoughts seek oxygen, and wait for a yawn to help
Me inhale, and for the gland to Secrete its magic.
Thirsty, my cells drink the wet moisture within,
Allowing the new air to cool the dryness in my heart.
As I feel like as anonymous desert, abandoned in
Time where distance and being have no bearing,
And my journey in space and time has been
Marred in a nothingness of pain.
As only the cries of human history, in a barren
land, scarred by despots and their greed will remain,
And the shrill of blood, splashed against the horizon
Will blare, as caged children with hollowed eyes, in
Askance will stare, hungry for their human flare.

Manifest Destiny

You are so violent and hateful; what does your
venom say, in your vile tandem bray of your holy
Christian Say, crushing nature on its way,
Leaving battle dead instead, where sardonic
Despots lay hungry bodies on their trays as
their greedy instincts pry on the weak without
dismay, and, the starving children cry with their
Bellies to the sky, bloating, floating with much
grief, while greedy fingers tear and / grab our
intestines, bones and flesh, as their lustful
Copious hearts / preach of Heaven and not
      Earth... making it a human waste.

A Seance

A short cut to silence
A silence without breath
A breath with a quiet echo
An echo without eyes
Eyes without glimmer
A glimmer without a soul
A soul without a body
A body without a lung
A lung gasping for breath
A breath without gills
A fish without a stream
A stream without a flow
A vacuum of stars
Lightless stars glistening,
And a wordless body at
Peace without words:
in an ocean of
nothingness, bathing...

Tone Deaf

Mesmerized with silence and prayer, I fold my
words into twisted forms, unable to visualize
the seas of time, and like hands knotted
in fate...
whose destiny is to repeat humanity's
holocaustic atrocities, I shiver in shame
that I've embrace the idea that god is greed, and
that his blessing is with you only if you want
more.

How alien have the gifts of nature become;
our forest ablaze because the thirst for
electricity has run amuck, as neon signs
advertise housing developments into
meadows and grass lands, and soon enough
to the ocean's bottoms where fish exist,
leaving
more ghettos
                behind.

How alien has a simple breath become when
its pulse is felt and revered, only if a cell
phone is in a palm, and the ear drum no
Longer hums the quiet melodies of heart.

How can I pray to silence when the heavy
metal of commercialism grips the essence of
my teeth, and the body shrivels in a smog of
despair: unable to sing the melodies of the
vowels; its gums stripped from the consonants
of hope, as the Christian Taliban carves at my
Soul, and silence and prayer no longer exist.

Obituary to the Merced Brave

The sound of my blood gurgles; it wants to talk to me.
However, my inner ear rejects its echo, and its sound
Drowns in my throat. Richard Silva, Lee Greenwood,
Steve Benson, Todd Hawkins, Tommy Bass, Woody Winslow,
Peter Martinez, Ruben Garcia, Benny Verduzco, Ollie
Carradine, Stuart Rowe, Ronnie Hall, Mike Buelna,
Larry Anderson, Laval Winzer and little brother Freddy,
Don Smith, Joe & Baby Marques, John Garcia, Carlos
Martinez, George and Ray Brice, Paul Brown, Peter Duran,
Henry & Johnny Broughten, Joe Reyes and, so many
Others that live within...

My blood wants to speak about them; it wants to make
Amends with them. It wants to reach out to them, and
Apologize for not understanding them, for not telling
Them they were poets in the stars and brothers in a red
Line of poverty that hampered our human sense. I was
Unable to speak to them, and instead saw them as entities
To be feared or envied.

Suspicion and competition reeked through our bones.
And our brotherhood in time gave way to a foul aroma.
A make believe system called second class, and striving
To climb out of it, we were drained, damaged, and almost
Destroyed, but our astuteness helped us through: Danny
Barnes, Clifford Greenwood, Nash Lopez, Eddie Garcia
Richard Krumm, Benny Valdez, Johnny Domingues and
Ray Trabucco became our role models, and we followed.

And, surviving our human plight / as time will be our witness,
We will, in the memory of our descendants live in honor.
As the poets that we were: and they will see that we
Shadow boxed...
That our quick feet, our grace, and flaming faith prepared
Them for a real encounter called life, leaving them a brief
Smell of flowers that we planted for them.

Stranded

The yawn, verve of an inhaling cornea
Seeking carbon dioxide in the motion
Of faraway pastures dotted with clouds.
Then disappearing quickly, leaving
The eyelash stunned in despair/ without
A picture of sound that the teeth can
Taste, savor nor hear, as the brutal nouns
And pronouns of greed seal the retina
With desperate sounds of paranoia
Terrorizing the mind, stranding the body
In stifling attention; startled in silence.

El Benny V.

The sky darkened, and there was a bang, a bullet
fractured the skull, as a train quickly swept by
Afterwards, the Santa Fe, leaving plumes of smoke:
Faces appeared, Eddie Garcia, Carlos Martinez,
Joe Berumen, Joe Sarabia, Mike Miramontes,
Danny Ornealas, and a host of others, whose chatter
Buzzed in a gaiety of Sound.
Big Benny had decided to join them; He would lead
Them in Do Wops again, their voices echoing clear
In the galaxies of light, flashing Memories of love and
Laughter on to us with their booming smiles.
Benny Valdez, the Barrio Boy who had all of what
Capitalism had to offer on this Earth, and yet rejected it,
as it did not heal the wounds that the system had
Had inflicted on his mother, Bernice and Brother, Eloy.

Benny Valdez, our hero, our brother, and at times leader,
We now weep for you. If only you would have
Accepted our love...perhaps it would have been different.
(The sky cleared in silence after the bang, Left with another
shinning star, as The train (Saintly Faith) sauntered past
G Grade). And, as we now stand holding our hearts in
Our hands in tribute to you... Vaya con Dios Benny,
    Your star will always burn brightly in us.

11/14/2:
to a cherished friend and his family

Making America Grim Again & Again

Manifast Destiny (aka Maga)
Your fingers of death grips
The uvula of humanity,
Never enough is the motto.
The Indian Holocaust for the
lands occupied by the Stone
Age people of the America
Continents.
The slave trade / to work
Those lands after the native
annihilation. And, reaching
California / more massacare /
Killing one hundred forty
Five thousand indigenous
In a mere fifty years, and now
one hundred & twenty-three
later / Democracy... you
have been a reaper
                    Since 1492.

Bear Creek

Your eyes are the shadows of the town; Bear Creek...
your meandering flow carved deltas, marshes and low lands,
where sea birds arrived to marvel your creation;
your eyes loomed omnipotently in the moon's radiance, glowing
vibrantly on the land, before your shadow became a
darkness, and you slept...

Nourishing the macrocosms, as they fertilized your belly,
which extended like finger to Franklin Road, curving to McSwain,
past the back roads of Atwater to Livingston, and on to your
destiny: emptying into the Merced that then carried you to
the San Joaquin and into the Delta, the Bay and finally to
the Pacific.

Your Native Sons, the Indigenous: looking for duck, pheasant,
geese, blackberries and pine nuts, came to visit you for their
nutrients, and to cool off in the current of your flow, before
departing your hot summer home, The Valley.

It was as if the Gods had chosen you; it was like if Bear Creek
Camp became your soul; like if you had waited for the Fierro, the
Gallego, The Banda, The Ramirez and Garcia families that gave
life to Chente, Ricardo, Beto, el Firocha, el Monchi and las rucas
suaves; la Rosemary, la Nancy and la Pewee, and those other clans
that gave birth to your town, Merced... Doing the labor for your
neon lights, and houses that arose from the Banks.

Bear Creek... A wonder for us that inherited your splendor;
a history that gravitates to the sea, carrying the vibrant beats of the
Martin Campos Parra Band who serenaded it. Bear Creek, a
movement of the heart for the people above your banks, and those
who swam in your muddy waters with delight.

Decibels

Decibels of sound, grinding teeth of anxiety,
How you filter through my bones, causing
Doubt and terror in my heart's eye, scalding
The infinity of my be with a burning blindness.
My saliva is my only pathway to you, and so I
Eat, chewing in vain to hear the song of
nature in you, but blinded by a beautiful
blue sky that glows in the light of day, stuns
me deaf.

One track mind my wife says I am, as lately
The only decibel I can hear is her voice
Telling me that why don't I listen to her that
After all it is for my own good, as I cannot
Seem to take care of myself. I wrecked my
Car the other day after golfing; another accident,
Her voice replied in a silent scowl when I told
her.

I tell her that I am looking for decibels,
To hear the passion of the real me that is missing
In time and space, and in the center of my
Minds eye. I am looking for cadence I tell her,
that perhaps then I can experience the gravity
of sound and light simultaneously.

She says that I spent too much time in coffee
Shops talking to the wrong people... that I
Should have learned how to work more instead
of living in the abstract; that while other friend's
widows will have nice retirements; she will have
none; I tell her that there is a house that she can sell
and she grunts; my shoulder joints cringe
/her decibels become mine and I ponder her well
Being.

The clear blue sky blazes in beauty, and a smoke
of sound curls in my palms as I write
and shutter in fragile desbelief...
thinking I will live forever.

The Violent one Percent

Keeping an impression in the raw,
In the hollow reaches of the vein, in
The startled moment of the heart,
And in a quiet morning light:
Before a raking sun enters and,
The window of the eye is disturbed
By the hazard of the day / And its
Soul begins to tremble to the horrid
Shades of time, as its pulse of life
Gets tangled in the sand storms of
The mind, and its ear drum
Becomes Frozen in the pitch-less
Thud of crime, as its startled
Breath gets smothered by the lies
Of neon lights, as the wealthy
Keep on Trumping: in its pimping
Ways of mime, and the people
Keep on slaving...
As the same of yesteryear, and
Their moan is not a ballet, but a
Shout of shrieking pain: of humanity
Gone sour, for greed has gone
Too far, as the instincts writhe in
Horror for the future of Mankind.

Blade & Spade

A word cannot live in space; its
Too heavy to exist; Yet, it cannot
Be allowed to sink...
To the bottom of the ocean floor
To a Davy Jones of yore.

As a word like a stream must
Flow and, decode its fluid's glow
Stirring ripples in its waves while
Spreading pictures with much
Glare; daring its spinal flair
To create magic carpets in the
Air, reflecting pebbles with much
care.

As in a breeze called Jorge, a
Metaphor, a shinning blade, an
Eternal
Flaming
Blaze,
Skirling bravely in its gaze.
A fearless consonant with a tired
Back, thinking that no dream,
Is too burdensome to fling.

At a heaven far and wide with a
Potent human might; whirling
Vowels as he yawns, vigorously
toward the sky, his children being
is only sight when heaving
mountains of much weight with
  His poetic Language Spade.

To the blade, el Superman,
Jorge Verdugo

We Are The Sun

The bite and venom of the moment, a
A flash of light, an explosion of silence,
And the mind like an empty hand goes
blank; only a magnetic hush hovers.
Today / There are no shadows; only
Pebbles beneath a stream, bright like
A rainbow, transparent to the seas...

Where the inhaling organs waken and sigh.
A blessing that only a seepage of breath
And the glance of an eye can see, as
Nature, the splendor of a rose, blooms
The sweet taste of green grass, and an
Aroma of wonder surges where invisible
Bones dance in silence.

The noise and excitement of the
Nervous system stirs and the burble of
The blood, purple red glows, and the
Lost matter of the brain battles the mercantile,
And the wants and desires of a society
That inhales the mercenary materials
Needed for an eternity that does not exist.

Silence and sound torn from its roots
Surges gushingly in response: and the
senses kindle in delight, without noise,
mesmerized by the moment and, the curving
glint of a stream that empties...
                    Into a river of thought.

I live in fear

Between the space of a vowel
and a consonant, a silent scream
wakes my parasympathetic network,
And, chaos and delirium set in. I
lay in terror wondering why its echo
has not shattered my skull to pieces;
My only defense to it is to sing and
yawn, and at that I do both badly.
Besides my ear is not trained to
hear, nor feel the ecstasy in my
lung... Lances and spears pierced
it, and it became a sin to inspire
& expire in my desire to be free.
Regardless, I find myself
addicted to space and its exploding
silence that like a shattered star
disperses to my feet, and all I can do
is run; but its invisible thunder
seizes me still, and, I float in stationary
fear, unable to move, gasping for a
language or / an image that can ease
the crashing noises that seek
words of peace and hope / that can
settle the roar and thunder that
waken the furies of a rabid history
That perforates my human soul.
A language where silence is not
a crime, but a seance where the
gargle of a brook streams over rocks
in the morning sun; and/whose soft
hum mazes through like an
ocean stealing into the sands of mother
earth; seeking to speak fearless and
clear: to the bosom of the universe.

To My Homeboys Trapped in Prison

The Meadows of the Mind

I must allow the vibration of my pulse to glide in
Its panorama of thought, so that the bones can
understand the magnitude of their moment, before
it aggravatingly gyrates in procrastination and
terror; I must understand Its fifteen second grace
period where the brain rests from the present,
And orbits.
Where it can dwell in the waters of sound and
like glittering gold fish, reflect brightly in the sun
inhaling its rays, smelling.
Where the shadows of doubt and cynicism do
not sour nor blemish its notions and emotions,
where transparent syllables of breath can find
harmony in the clarity of its moment...
And not allow the sins of man to defecate the
world with hate and, permit the mind to gleam with
the vision of its glow... to shine in nature's gleam,
where we can become a united human race, and
history's rot will no longer pierce our feet and
palms, with its with its nails of misery / and the
meadows of the mind can resurrect in an echo,
floating in time.

Hero Students of 1969

I die in strange roadways;
my body slumped in contorted
positions in car lots and
shopping malls where manicured
fingernails reach for my soul
and...
Give me change in return.
I die in shadows surrounded
By mirrors where voices
Nibble on sweet bread
And bitter coffee, where
Mohammed Ali mumbles
Still about freedom.
I die in a mysterious
Vacuum where the afternoon
Requisites love and,
The furies of time
Assault it instead.
I die where the sea no
longer touches the sky and its
Waves rage
In a purgatory of dreams.
I die in alley ways where
Echos of Huarache-less feet
Trample over me and shouts
Of "Only in America," Smother
My lungs.
I die haunted by the Year
1969, as Television Children
Drag their parents down fast
Food highways and Hector
Cortez, accompanied by
Steve Solano, sing...
       "Yo Soy Chicano."

To Eddie Arano, and all the
Fresno State in coming EOP
Students of 1969

Trapped in Space

Terrorized by the present, his yawn...
Trapped in the crevice between the
Teeth and gum suffocates; the
Hippocampus writhes in silent despair,
As the echo of the eardrum, muffled
By the by sternum closes the pupil of
The eye, though, the sensations of
The sun's rays warm his skin,   he is
Paralyzed, perplexed & paranoid.
The words that are supposed to clarify
His humanity... are like passing
clouds, and unless they bring rain to
This thirsty and hot Valley, they are
meaningless.
He stares emptily at the blank space of
His computer, looking to see if he can
Conjure up syllables, phonemes, and
Other waves of sound that will unite
Him with the yawn, thinking... why is
It so difficult for his imagination to
Breathe freely and to visualize the
                    The echos of his mind?

To My Grandson Ceasar Feliciano

Un Amigo

The mist of time evaporates, followed by a
shower of thought.... Waddel Antonio Gallegos
has past. Though, his vibrance is felt by the
many who knew and loved him. Antonio
Waddel, a brilliant person whose association
with language at a young age, empowered
him to overcome the daunting challenges of
poverty. His ability to perceive the future rested
in his temples, and in his quick moving eyes.
A gift inherited from his mother, Ursula, and
father, Fidel: both descendants of a Celtic vision
and a hearty Mexican determination.

The early dawn was his friend and will
remember him in his gangling gait, A Vato Loco
one, leading his brothers Orlando and Joe to
pick up Mikie Buelna, Myself, and meeting up
with el Porky Vargas, and Hector Verduzco to
 gather boxes in the alleys of 16th, 17th and 18th
streets to sell to the food markets in the town of
Merced. Then when daylight broke, the group
would stroll with shoe shine boxes in hand, going
from bar to bar barking shine, shoe shine sir
to patrons who were morning loungers at the
local bars, while waiting for the afternoon ones
to come.

He and his brothers were survivalists: work was
a matter of life for them. Dawn will also remember
them when they reached their mid teens, walking
in a mist of cold to 16th Street to get on buses that
took people to the fields where work made for
men awaited them: cotton to pick and chop, as
well as bell peppers, tomatoes, peaches, and
what not to be harvested.

Waddel Antonio... my friend. My tears a tribute
to your strength and perseverance. Adiós.

It Never Ends

Write to the curiosity
Of silence, and to the
Splendor of being
Alive... to that ripple
That swells in the
Eyes of your lungs,
And in the vibration of
Its echo, so to design
A figure that mirrors
The smile in your eyes.

La Domis, Sheila Gallardo

How time has interned in your
Body...
               Fascinates me,
How the movement of your thought
Puzzles me? You are an aspiration
Of my past hopes that wandered
In mindless shadows and revolting
Pulsations. When I see you walk in
your silent splendor, and in the
Kindred nature that time has given
You, I rile in stunned delight hearing
Your footsteps... in the echo of my
Heart.

A Troubled Lover

I write poems to remember and to forget.
The sun has warmed the morning; it
Was cold earlier; frost had sprinkled the
Valley Floor, and its grasses,
And grounded earth were covered in ice.

It was dark shadows curtained the sky,
And the stars were not visible, as dark
Clouds hovered. It was a cold
Troubling morning, but it is always like
That when you have children,
Grandchildren, and great grandchildren /

Love takes over, and the gnashing
Emotion that
You felt when you met your wife: the
Exhilaration, the blood thickening, as it
Tried to breathe, and the frozen body
That halted in a shutter when you
First saw her...

Has now multiplied, and you are now,
Even
More mesmerized,
Further in her Web; you pause for answers
But there are none, love is like that.

One cannot forget to remember; your
Moment lives on in her charm, her
Footsteps, and in her off springs, / and you
Are troubled...
                 You must protect that love.

No Oxygen Left

Taste the moment, its ether of light;
Then find the words that will help you
Inhale it. For one must visualize
his space, his horizon, so to taste
The fluids of his heart / and the pulse
That swims within, for Humanity is
At risk.
          The fish out of
Water is drowning in his spit,
Terrified at its taste, unable to smell
Its pitch, tribalism's hate hovers; its
Booming rage drowns out the
     The echo of his crescendo.

Consumerized

I have become afraid to taste my thoughts.
It is a fear I learned, as cavernous
Hands reached out, to tear the Trinity in me:
I have become a feckless nuance, a shade
without a tree; my echos, and impressions:
torn away from me.
                        The hands distrust my
sense of touch, and are strangers to my be.
The gurgles of the ocean waves, a distance
from my sea, and so I hearken towards
their water's roar...
a forbidden tune to me, as gargles of saliva
regurgitate in me.

A river full of spittle, without a song to sing,
A pond shredded by fingers, whose hands
will never cease. Their god... in heaven
looking down at me, as its henchmen shred
my soul; it is not enough I suffer / but must
bellow to my grave, and dying I'm so
angry that I tell my pedigree...
to eat the fruits of labor, and struggle,
                                to be free.

A Peace Offering

The echo should not have a
vowel; it should have space,
and, an eternal distant gaze,
guided by motion... where the
yawn of its waking silence is
wonder, and the majesty of its
howl, a shower of light rain
on a forest and, where words
become a vehicle for peace.

A seance where a body of
wind can glide in the gravity of
a human touch.
A place where the music of the
blood can sing the voices of the
universe with transparent words
with eyes... / that speak about
eternity and / of the grace and
and splendor of being alive, not
the hate spewed by the autocrat
class.

Taming The Day

As I inhale the melody of life,
I try to listen to my palms, where
The glottis and the pupils of the
Eye meet, (to feels the flavors of
Of one's purview), and where
The flowing of the glands sprout
Like sluices, gurgling into song,
Forcing the gums/
        To yawn in harmony.

The nervous system has rested.
The rosters have cocked the
Doodle day from its darkness
And the search for food and
Substance has begun.

What pitch of flavors water in
My mouth, and what echos of
Sound filter through my throat,
While nothingness touches
My knuckles & spine.

Carefully... I wrestle my back
Against the chair, and slowly curl
My hands to massage them,
And to protect my skeletal joints
From wayward notes that may
Touch them and ruin their day.

I must not allow monoxide gas
To touch my teeth. I must
Exhale through my eyes, and let
The intervals of space, the
Photons, quantum theory might
Say, spread musingly, so that
They can gaze forever in the
Music of time, and in a
        Splendor called taste.

Finite expression

A yawn should negate verse,
Removing the rhyme, the
meter...
The cadence, and even the
Idea and word: until only
the poem
is left, and the glow of its
flow explodes
Into a consonant of sound
Where its vowel
Becomes a mirage
And / the vapor of its echo,
The conducting hand that
makes
        A sad worlds sing.

The lost Chemical

The chemical filters to my neurons. It sparkles,
making my glands savor my thoughts; nonetheless,
I am tired despite the fact that I just woke. Normally
I would be thrilled, as I have found the dark hour to
be my best friend. It is when I talk to nature. It is
when my mind finds the courage to look inward; to
speak to my body and brain cells, seeking counsel
from them as to how to handle my day when light
floods the landscape & when the sins of the world
come at me unceasingly aggressive: when people
are angry for having to wake up, and are anxious to
let me know that I am the Fault of It, speaking
harshly to me in foreign tongues.

They say that I don't know my place, and zoom past
me in fast automobiles, cursing because something
is wrong with my skin color; it is my fault that they
have to work, I was supposed to take care of them
for life; I am a descendant of their nannies,
Their cooks, their farm laborers, their railway builders?

I am not allowed to gaze at their manicured houses,
with shrubs imported from the tropics, and they honk
Their shiny car horns when I do. What are you
Doing here anyway, is added? Go back to where you
Come from. Yet the chains on my ankles and neck don't
Allow it.
They have raped my countries and lands, taken them over.

I have no place to go, and they are angry that I haven't
Died for their sins like I was supposed to. As a result, I
Like dark mornings because they hide me from daylight.
Their quiet allows me to breathe in peace, to seek
That which thrives in the dopamine chemical required by
the neurons that spark the motion required by the
Gravity of the stars, that internal radiation that makes
one human, as I search for its love; the love that was
torn from humanity by the immorality of more: That
Now threatens the existence of all of earth's children.

A body in crises

I travel in a cloud of thought,
watching the river called life
flow by; time has made me
old, and my hands curl up
on a moments notice; my wife
says that it is carpal tunnel
because I work at the computer
too long, but I disagree, as !
think that I over annihilated,
seeking the pleasures of my
youth.
A truly unfortunate situation;
but I must keep mum in
shame for trying to slow time
down in a grasp of
       disappointment.
My hands must be my hands,
as that is all I have left, For my
feet are pained with arthritis,
and my shoes do not fit anymore
and I have to wear Huaraches
again, which are bad for my feet,
especially in cold Winter
       mornings.

Growing Flowers

Fifteen seconds, they writhe
anonymously; only your glands
know they exist; they sing; reflecting
The elements of a world that blind you.
The odors of the flowers terrify you,
and you lie in the dark, and you
Dream...
     Time is real. Your organs become
You in motion, and you journey.
     Your soul becomes one with the
universe, fear and delight mingle,
and you are afraid; You do not
hear, but you are able to see; your
deceased mother holds you in
her arms, And you see yourself
Smile, Securely and Warm.
     However, the smell of flower that
was her, is absent, and you weep:
waking to a dawn, seeking the echo
of her love; Looking for the garden
hat she Planted in you, And you
stumble wounded, unable to see her,
but you know she's there: in the
footsteps of time and in the meadows
of your heart growing flowers.

Sheila

Forty years evaporated, but like clouds
in a deep blue sky you remained. Your
timeless gaze, the warm look that has
kept our family safe, and the love that
reflects from your pupils, fills our hearts
and mine / with an eternity that only a
vein can drink. A vein that glows rose
red, A vein that streams in a sunset
gleaming in the sea, fighting the night
for one last look at you before the dawn.
Forty years, my Babe, thank
you for this transparent time, and for the
children you have blessed me with.

to my wife

In Wait

I color myself in blue; not because
I am sad. It is because in the blue
Of the night, the skies glisten in the
Darkness of thought with clear
vision; vaporizing the heart with
New ways to aspire, as descending
Songs of the eye fill the lungs with
Chimeras of forgotten oceans,
Its waves washing over the images
Of the day: busy shopping and
Looking for love where none exists,
Or hoping that the day can heal the
Wounds of humankind...
That is why I go to bed early, so to
Wait for the blue of the night, and
Wait for the arms of my deceased
Mother and,
Feel the hope of her warmth

Anxiety on Hold

Bewildered by the silence of time, the moment
disassembles itself, scattering fugaciously in
an ephemeral and evanescent wind of darkness
whose sweeping force leaves a wounded hollow
in the cavity of thought: a blindness and a
swelling in the pith of its heart: an anxiety
caused by anxieties whose currents
drift and quiver / undefined by weightless words
that flee in rapid tides, seeking clarity in the
waves of an ocean,
      Swaying in the glare of a roaring moon.

To my grand & great grandchildren

Speaking in Particles

Seeking for crevices that blend into
half steps, quarter notes, eighths
and sixteenth notes, and to hold
time in your palm, as its motion
becomes an illusion, but where its
blood flow, nonetheless, continues
gurgling, seeking truth in harmony
and rhyme & in the particles of light,
in a mirror of sound called

                    perception.

A place where the annuals of self-
destruction: created by the chosen
ones, the self anointed (those who
crave gold teeth & who gobble on
gizzards and falsehoods), squeeze
the heart beat of humanity with
non existent rainbows of greed and
delusion, where the magnetic wave
of existence is warped by a dark
rage called the I and the me,
scattering image less photons, and
the essences of the pulse suffers
in blind exhaustion and despair.

Body & Time

Pleasing, praying and silence, impressions,
Behavior, curiosity, thought and wonder.
A dust storm of space time overcomes the
impulses, and swirling images flare from
Swollen cavities, flushed with a kaleidoscope
Of flavors unleash terrorized glands that
Seize the body mute; speechless to the
many taste buds to tend to, as horizons too
vast to encompass: where subterranean
rivers flow require a shift back to nature, and
allow the touch of time to speak, and the
notion of the veins to be free again, so that
The eyes can bask in the enameled
language of space, and time can deal with
the profound significance of the moment,
and the naked word can define the
                    symphony of the moment...

Unhurried Nth

An unhurried moment; the passing
of the now; leaving an eternal symphony
of sound that transpire into images
of unending pitches and horizons,
where the fibers of light bend/forming
nourishing fluids that circulate quietly
in a nth of splendor; celebrating
taste, smell and the touch of mountain
tops and valleys with the blink of
an eye, as the cornea in subtle
resonance inhales the beauty of a
        Autumn waiting to bloom.

The Yoga of Me

A breath becomes a sound or
Is it that a sound becomes a
A breath, and the pause to
Understand which, creates a
Decibel of Time; a moment of
Space where taste & smell
Seep through its crevices to
Discover touch, and the eye
Can reflect patiently to decipher
The echo of that resonance...
And touch the quiet of your
Bones.

About the Author

Rudy Gallardo was born in 1940 in La Aldea, Guanajuato to a Chichimeca mother. At the age of five his family migrated to Brawley, California, but after a short stay, they then moved to Tracy. Later, beacause work was more plentiful, the family settled in the town of Merced in the central San Joaquin Valley. There, Rudy attended Galen Clark, Margret Sheehy and Herbert Hoover schools, graduating from Merced High in 1958. After graduation, he attended City College of San Francisco for a semester, where he participated in a student boxing competition, and won the fighter of the night medal. Before that he was runner up in the Northern California Golden Gloves Tournament, winning a silver buckle. While stationed in Wildflecken, Germany, a battalion of the Third Army Division, protecting the border against the Soviet Union in the 2nd of the 15th Mechanized Infantry, he was part of the Division's boxing. But realizing that looking for prestige in beating up people was not in him, quit boxing.

After his Army two-year tour ended on May 22nd, 1964, he returned to his job at Foster Farms in Livingston, California, and seriously started his search for his humanity and self-worth. During his employment there, he attended Merced College part-time and received his A.A. Degree in 1967. Then transferring to Fresno State, Professors like Philip Levine, Eugene Zumwalt, Gene Bluestein, Lilian Faderman, Charles Hanzlicek, Peter Everwine, and their very humanistic English Department inspired him to seek his worth and humanity in community organizing and writing. He has initiated publications for the Central San Joaquin Valley's bilingual population: *Sentimientos del Valle, El Amigo Noticiero, La Voz del Centro, El California*, and was a pioneer in helping develop *El Telocote Newspaper* in San Francisco. He, Jorge Garcia, Omar Salinas, Morris Martinez, Oscar Acosta, Guillermo Martinez, Yolanda Diaz, Lina Mares, Dolores Hernandez and Victoria Chacon, as students at Fresno State, organized a state-wide student group to lobby for the Educational Opportunites Program, which currently helps low-income families to send their kids to College.

Dr. Jorge Garcia